SCIENCE AND SOCIETY™

ANIMAL TESTING

ISSUES AND ETHICS

Stephanie Watson

ROSEN
PUBLISHING®

New York

Published in 2009 by The Rosen Publishing Group, Inc.
29 East 21st Street, New York, NY 10010

Copyright © 2009 by The Rosen Publishing Group, Inc.

First Edition

Library of Congress Cataloging-in-Publication Data

Watson, Stephanie.
Animal testing : issues and ethics / Stephanie Watson.—1st ed.
    p. cm.—(Science and society)
Includes bibliographical references and index.
ISBN-13: 978-1-4358-5022-4 (library binding)
1. Animal experimentation—Moral and ethical aspects—Juvenile literature. I. Title.
HV4915.W38 2009
179'.4—dc22

                                        2008013415

Manufactured in Malaysia

On the cover: A lab researcher in China feeds white rats that are used in experiments for pharmaceutical research at a medical school.

CONTENTS

Morning sickness is one of the most unpleasant side effects that a woman experiences when she is pregnant. Women with morning sickness sometimes feel so nauseated that they can barely get out of bed. In the 1960s, when a drug was introduced that prevented morning sickness, many pregnant women jumped at the chance to take it. That drug was called thalidomide. What women didn't realize at the time was that thalidomide could cause serious birth defects if it was taken during pregnancy. Thalidomide was eventually banned from use, but only after about ten thousand babies around the world were born with missing arms and legs, according to the March of Dimes.

Thalidomide is a tragic example of a medicine causing serious harm. Today, the vast majority of drugs are safe, in large part because of the rigorous testing process they must go through before they can be approved for use by the public.

A big part of that testing process involves animals. Scientists try out new medicines and other treatments on animals to make sure they are safe enough to use on humans. Animal research has helped scientists develop lifesaving treatments for deadly diseases such as AIDS, cancer, and diabetes, and it has helped create vaccines to protect against polio, measles, mumps, and rubella—diseases that once killed millions of people. Testing with animals has also helped scientists learn which chemicals might be dangerous to people if they are swallowed, touched, or inhaled.

Yet, not everyone sees animal testing as a good method. Opponents say that the millions of animals that are involved in testing each year are being made to endure terrible pain and

Animal testing has helped scientists develop vaccines and treatments for many diseases that once killed millions of people, but animal rights groups are concerned that testing animals is not humane.

suffering, with little to no regard for their well-being. James M. Jasper and Dorothy Nelkin wrote in their 1991 book, *The Animal Rights Crusade*, that animals are being treated as nothing more than "test tubes with legs."

The Animal Testing Debate

Animal testing ignites very strong emotions on both sides of the debate. On one extreme end are people who believe that animals are human property to do with what people wish. On the other extreme end are those who believe that animals are equal to—or even above—humans in value and should not be used for any purpose, not even for food.

Surveys show that most people fall somewhere in between these two arguments. In a 2004 poll by the Gallup research company, almost two-thirds of Americans said they thought medical tests on animals were morally acceptable.

Most scientists also fall in the middle of the two opposing arguments. Although they believe it is important to test new treatments on animals, they are trying to use as few animals as possible and are trying to conduct the experiments as humanely as possible. To that end, they have been working hard to develop new methods for testing medicines and chemicals. Thanks to their efforts, it might one day be possible to test new treatments without having to experiment on a single animal.

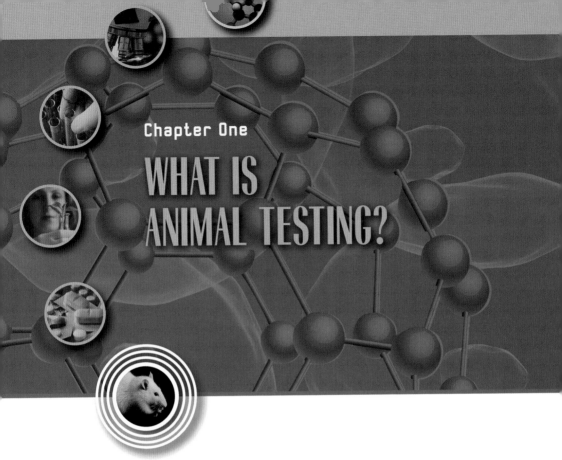

Chapter One

WHAT IS ANIMAL TESTING?

A nimals and humans have many biological similarities. Because of these similarities, scientists can find out how humans might react to medicines, cosmetics, chemicals, and other products by testing them on animals first.

More than twenty-five million animals are used in research, testing, and education each year, according to the Humane Society of the United States. The three main areas of animal testing are biomedical research, education, and product safety.

Biomedical Research

So that they can produce effective treatments for disease, scientists need to understand exactly how the human body works and how diseases affect the body. To learn about treating disease, researchers introduce bacteria, a virus, or other substance that causes disease in animals. Then, they watch what happens to the animals after they give those animals different medicines and therapies.

Animals naturally get many of the same diseases as humans (including cancer), and they often react in the same way as humans to medications. These are two reasons why scientists say animals make good models in studying whether treatments are safe and effective for people.

One example of how scientists are using animals to study disease is that of knockout mice. These mice aren't boxers, as the name might suggest. Instead, they have a gene (or genes) that is

This "nude" mouse has been genetically changed so that its immune system doesn't work as it should. Having a weaker immune system makes the mouse a good model for disease.

changed or "knocked out" so that the mice develop traits that they wouldn't normally have. The changed gene might cause the mice to get sick with diabetes, heart disease, cancer, or other illnesses. Researchers can then study the effects of different treatments they apply to the disease.

Sometimes, scientists use animal tissues to produce treatments such as vaccines or medicines. One way to make insulin, a drug used to treat people with diabetes, is by taking the hormone from the pancreas of cows and pigs.

Another area of biomedical research in which animals have proved to be very helpful is in studying surgical methods. Imagine being wheeled into the operating room and having the doctor say to you, "I've never tried this operation before, but don't worry, I'm hopeful it will turn out all right." Doctors have learned how to perform surgeries by trying them out on animals first. Organ transplants, for example, might not have been possible without the help of animals. French doctor Alexis Carrel (1873–1944), who won the 1912 Nobel Prize in Physiology or Medicine, perfected a technique to join blood vessels from a transplanted organ to the recipient's body by using dogs.

Biologist and surgeon Alexis Carrel was a pioneer in organ transplant surgery, thanks to techniques that he first tested out on dogs.

Education

By the time they reach high school, many students will have already dissected a worm, frog,

Dissecting a frog or other animal in biology class can help high school students learn about organs and how they work.

pig, or other animal in science class. This scientific experiment may not be the most pleasant experience, but it can help students learn about biology and discover what an animal's organs look like and how they work.

At colleges and universities, students majoring in science or medicine often examine animals—both alive and dead—to study how the body works. They might observe an animal's heartbeat or how its stomach digests food. They then apply what they've learned to the treatment of humans (or animals, if they're studying veterinary medicine).

Product Safety

Before any medicine can reach drugstore shelves, the U.S. Food and Drug Administration (FDA), a government agency, requires that it be tested on animals. If the drug appears to be safe and effective in animals, only then is it tested in human studies called clinical trials.

Animals also help scientists learn what effect chemicals might have on people's health if those chemicals are released into the air or water. Many companies test products such as makeup or skin lotion to make sure they won't cause allergies or other reactions when humans use them.

Early History of Animal Testing

Animals have been helping doctors study diseases and their possible treatments for centuries. Although animal experiments may have been done even earlier in history, the Greeks were the first to record their animal tests.

In 450 BCE, the Greek philosopher Alcmaeon of Croton performed the first recorded vivisection (cutting open a living animal) when he severed the optic nerve in a dog's eye. Although the experiment sounds gruesome, it helped doctors at the time understand why people become blind. The Greek philosopher Aristotle (384–322 BCE) and the physician Erasistratus (304–258 BCE) both reportedly performed tests on live animals.

A Roman physician named Claudius Galen (c. 129–150 CE) learned about nerves and muscles by dissecting pigs, goats, and other animals. For his work, Galen became known as the Father of Vivisection.

Centuries later, British surgeon William Harvey (1578–1657) learned how the blood moves through the body by looking inside animals. His work encouraged more scientists in Europe to use animal vivisection for research. Dutch scientist Antoni van

Leeuwenhoek (1632–1723) observed animal tissues under the microscopes he developed.

Many of the most famous breakthroughs in history were due to work with animals. In 1796, the English doctor Edward Jenner (1749–1823) took pus from a cow infected with cowpox. Then, he injected it into a boy's arm, paving the way for the first vaccine against the deadly disease smallpox. French chemist Louis Pasteur (1822–1895) pioneered the use of vaccines for anthrax, cholera, and rabies in sheep, chicken, and other animal test subjects.

Philosophies on Animal Testing

Do animals have a soul? Do they feel pain? And do they deserve to be treated with equal respect as humans? These are some of the questions at the heart of the animal testing debate.

Some philosophers throughout history have believed that animals rank far below humans in the evolutionary hierarchy (ranking). Thomas Aquinas (1225–1274), an Italian philosopher and theologian, argued that animals cannot reason and were created by God solely for human use. French philosopher René Descartes (1596–1650) considered animals as nothing more than machines with no soul or ability to feel pain. "The greatest of all the prejudices we have retained from our infancy is that of believing that the beasts think," he said, according to a translation of his writings entitled *The Philosophical Works of Descartes*.

On the other side of the debate was English philosopher Jeremy Bentham (1748–1832), who believed that animals such as horses and dogs were every bit as rational as a human child, if not more so. "The question is not, 'Can they reason?' nor, 'Can they talk?' but rather, 'Can they suffer?' " He predicted, "The time will come when humanity will extend its mantle over everything which breathes," according to the book *Law Relating to Animals* by Simon Brooman.

Centuries later, two men helped launch the modern idea of animal rights. In the 1970s, the Australian philosopher Peter

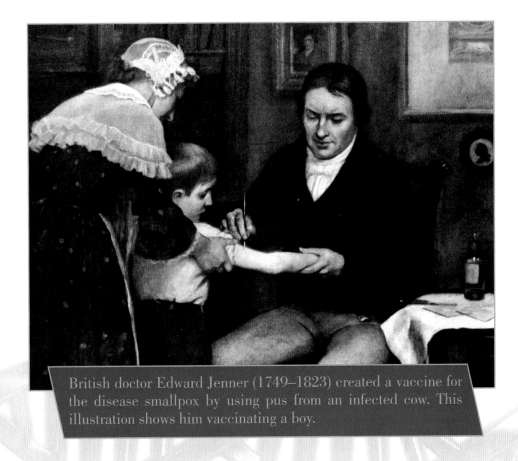

British doctor Edward Jenner (1749–1823) created a vaccine for the disease smallpox by using pus from an infected cow. This illustration shows him vaccinating a boy.

Singer (1946–) wrote a book entitled *Animal Liberation*, which is considered the bible of the animal rights movement. Singer considered animal research as being as morally wrong as racism. He believed that all species of animal—man, ape, dog, or mouse—deserve equal respect. "From an ethical point of view, we all stand on an equal footing—whether we stand on two feet, or four, or none at all," Singer wrote in his 1985 book, *In Defense of Animals*.

American philosophy professor Tom Regan (1938–) also argued for the rights of animals. He said those rights include the need to be treated with respect by humans and not to be used simply as tools in scientific experiments.

Magendie and Bernard

If animals can feel pain and suffer as Bentham and other philosophers suggested, then the experiments of two French scientists in the 1800s would have been unbearably painful to their subjects. French scientists François Magendie (1783–1855) and Claude Bernard (1813–1878) made great scientific strides with their research. However, some people were not happy about the way the two scientists conducted their experiments.

When Magendie started performing his animal experiments at the College of France in the early 1800s, he didn't use any pain-relieving medicine (anesthesia) on the animals because it didn't exist at the time. In one study, Magendie opened the skin in the backs of several puppies and cut the nerves of their spinal cords. Then, he watched as the puppies lost the ability to move and became paralyzed. This experiment helped Magendie learn about the function of nerves.

At the time, many people were horrified by Magendie's techniques. One English doctor who watched Magendie's experiments in 1837 called them "revolting," as recounted in F. Barbara Orlans's book *In the Name of Science: Issues in Responsible Animal Experimentation*.

Claude Bernard was Magendie's student and later his assistant. After Magendie died, Bernard continued his teacher's animal experiments. In one study, Bernard gave curare to rabbits, dogs, and frogs. Curare is a very strong poison that causes the muscles to become paralyzed. Bernard dissected the animals' nerves and muscles to discover what effect the poison had on them.

Bernard justified his work with animals in the name of medical research. "No hesitation is possible: the science of life can be established only through experiment, and we can save living beings from death only after sacrificing others," Bernard said, according to *In the Name of Science*.

Many people believe that Bernard and Magendie made great contributions to the field of medicine. However, anger over their

The Food, Drug, and Cosmetics Act

In 1937, more than one hundred Americans, many of them children, died after taking a medicine to treat bacterial infections. Scientists later discovered that the medicine had been tainted with the deadly poison diethylene glycol (which is a liquid used in car antifreeze, among other products).

The company that produced the drug hadn't known that the drug was dangerous because it had never tested it. The diethylene glycol tragedy led President Franklin Roosevelt to sign the Food, Drug, and Cosmetics Act in 1938. The act required that companies prove to the FDA that their drugs were safe before selling them. Much of that proof came from performing animal tests.

animal experiments was so intense that it led to the beginning of the antivivisection movement in Europe.

LD50 and Draize Test

As medical science progressed, animal testing became more common. In the early 1900s, scientists began to regularly test drugs such as insulin (a hormone given to diabetics to control blood sugar levels) to make sure that each batch had the same strength and effectiveness.

The test scientists used for this purpose was developed in 1927 by a British biologist named J. W. Trevan (1887–1956). It was called LD50, which stood for "lethal dose 50 percent." Researchers gave each drug to groups of ten animals, often rats. The goal was to find out how high the dose had to be to kill 50 percent, or half, of

Scientists are using these mice to study a hormone that might one day help humans lose weight.

the animals. This experiment helped researchers learn what dose would be toxic (poisonous) to humans. A single LD50 test killed hundreds of animals.

Another test that came into use during the mid-1900s was the Draize eye test. It was named after its developer, American scientist John Draize (1900–1992). He designed the test in 1944 as a way to find out whether products such as shampoo, hair spray, detergents, drugs, and pesticides would irritate or damage the eyes.

The Draize test uses albino (colorless) rabbits. Their large, clear eyes make it easy for scientists to see any damage or irritation. During the Draize test, scientists place the test chemical in one of the rabbit's eyes. Over a period of several days, the scientists watch what happens to that eye as compared to the other, untreated eye.

Both the LD50 and Draize tests proved very controversial, and animal rights activists eventually demanded that they be halted. Some scientists have also spoken out against the test, saying that it is expensive and offers very little value to the research. Today, many companies have either stopped using the Draize test or are using far fewer animals in the test. The LD50 test has been banned in parts of Europe. In the United States, the Environmental Protection Agency (EPA) no longer supports the test's use; however, some companies still use the test outside of the United States.

Rabbits have large eyes, which help scientists who use the Draize test to study whether chemicals and cosmetics cause irritation or physical harm.

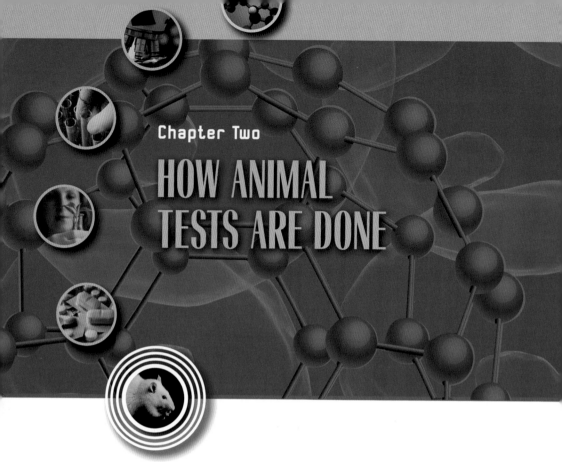

Chapter Two

HOW ANIMAL TESTS ARE DONE

esting begins when scientists develop a new chemical that they believe might help treat or cure a disease. Companies test drugs, chemicals, and sometimes cosmetics on animals to learn whether these products might be dangerous if people touch them, eat them, or breathe them in. Animal testing also helps researchers learn how much of the substance a person would need to be exposed to, and for what length of time, to cause the dangerous effects. One medication or product test might take three to four years to finish and cost a company several million dollars.

The first tests of a new substance might be done in test tubes to find out whether it is likely to be harmful or poisonous. Then, scientists will often use non-mammalian animals such as fish and worms to determine whether the chemical is safe enough to even produce. Finally, the substance is tested on mammals such as rats or mice.

If the product is designed to go inside a person's body (for example, if it is a medication that is taken by mouth), then scientists will look at its effects on all of the animal's organs over the length of that animal's entire life. They will also see what effects the substance might have on the animal's offspring.

Before a new medicine or chemical is tested on mice and other mammals, it is often tested on fish and other non-mammals to see whether it is safe.

What Products Are Tested

For the FDA to approve a new drug, that drug must first be tested on animals to make sure that it is safe for human use. The EPA also requires that chemicals be tested to make sure that they are not toxic to humans. Testing can be done on the finished product or on the ingredients. It can be performed by the company producing the substance, a laboratory, or the company that makes the ingredients.

The FDA does not require that companies test cosmetics. However, it does advise companies to use whatever methods (including animal tests) are needed to prove that the product is safe. Some cosmetics are tested to find out whether they might be toxic if swallowed or if they might cause eye and skin irritation, but many cosmetics companies today avoid the use of animal tests.

Dogs—and Chimps—in Space

Animals have not only been valuable to research conducted here on Earth. In the 1950s and 1960s, the United States and the Soviet Union were locked in the space race. Both nations were trying to be the first to make it to the moon. To reach that destination, they had to figure out how to launch a spacecraft out of Earth's orbit and into space. However, they were worried about the safety of sending humans into that unknown environment. Before the first humans were allowed to make the trip into space, scientists in both the American and Russian space

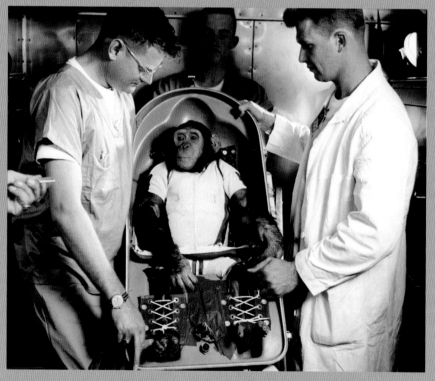

On January 31, 1961, a Mercury-Redstone rocket carrying Ham, a chimpanzee, was launched from Cape Canaveral, Florida. Ham became the first chimpanzee to travel into space.

programs wanted to make sure that animals could survive the weightlessness of living in zero gravity.

When the series of Russian *Sputnik* spacecraft were first launched in the 1950s, they were piloted by dogs. Laika, Belka, and Strelka were just a few of the canine pilots. On January 31, 1961, four months before Alan Shepard became the first human to travel into space, a chimpanzee named Ham made the journey. He survived his trip 157 miles (253 kilometers) above Earth's surface, including six minutes of weightlessness. After his journey into space, Ham retired in the Washington Zoo, where he lived until 1980.

Types of Animal Tests

Animal tests study how a chemical or drug is absorbed in the animal's body, moved through the body, and removed. One group of tests is based on the length of time the substance is given. Examples of these tests include the following:

- **Acute:** In these tests, the animal is exposed to the substance for less than one month. Acute tests are designed to see what effects a chemical will have if it touches a person's eyes or skin. If the substance is not meant to be eaten, then the tests will show what might happen if somebody accidentally puts it in his or her mouth. The Draize eye test is an example of an acute test.
- **Subchronic:** These tests observe an animal that has been exposed to a substance for a period of about three months to study the longer-term effects of a drug or chemical.

⟵◯ **Chronic:** These tests last for more than three months. They are designed to show the long-term effects of being exposed to the chemical. Long-term effects on an animal might include getting cancer or giving birth to offspring that have birth defects.

Tests also look at whether the substance does the following:

◯ Affects the animal's behavior or ability to think
◯ Causes cancer
◯ Damages the animal's cells or organs
◯ Burns, reddens, or causes rashes to form on the animal's skin
◯ Irritates the animal's eyes
◯ Affects the animal's ability to reproduce or leads to abnormal changes in the animal's offspring
◯ Kills the animal

If the product causes any of these effects on animals, then researchers know not to test it on humans.

Types of Animals That Are Used in Tests

Because mammals most closely resemble humans, they are the first choice for animal tests. Rats and mice make up 85 to 90 percent of all animals used in tests. Scientists say they use these animals because 80 percent of their genetic material—DNA—is identical to that of humans.

Mice are easy to work with in the lab for several reasons, including the following:

◯ They are small, making them easy to house.
◯ They have a lifespan of only two to three years, which allows scientists to study the effects of a drug or chemical on the mouse's body throughout the animal's entire life.

- They breed quickly and often. It takes from nineteen to twenty-one days for a female mouse to give birth, and she can have between five to ten litters per year.
- They are mild mannered.

Rabbits are also popular among scientific laboratories, both because they are easy tempered and because the old saying "breed like rabbits" is true. Rabbits can have from two to five litters per year, each of which can include between two and eight young. In 2002, nearly 250,000 rabbits were used in research in the United States, according to the U.S. Department of Agriculture (USDA). Rabbits are commonly used to study vaccines, as well as skin and eye irritation (for example, in the Draize test).

Although they were used more often for testing in the past, dogs, cats, and monkeys today make up only about 1 percent of all animal test subjects. Many of the monkeys used in experiments today are helping scientists study the disease HIV/AIDS because they can carry the virus.

Guinea pigs also used to play a bigger role in scientific experiments. You might have heard the phrase "to be a guinea pig," meaning "to serve as part of an experiment," but today very few animal tests actually involve the rodent.

Where Do Scientists Obtain Animals?

Most laboratory animals—mainly rats and mice—are bred for research by animal breeders. There are strict laws about which monkeys and other primates the laboratories can use because many apes are endangered.

Although millions of unwanted dogs and cats are put to sleep at shelters every year, the Humane Society is against the use of pound animals for this purpose. Most of the small number of dogs and cats that are used in research come from dealers. These dealers buy animals from their owners, from shelters, or from other dealers.

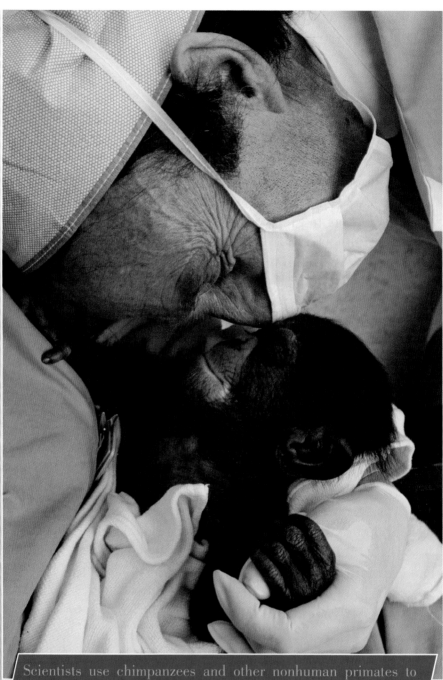

Scientists use chimpanzees and other nonhuman primates to help them develop new treatments for AIDS, a disease of the immune system.

What happens to the animals after the experiments are finished? Sadly, most animals are euthanized (killed in a humane way) after their experiments are finished so that scientists can see what effects the drugs or chemicals had on their tissues. A small number of animals are adopted or are put in refuges.

Animal Testing Laws

Even before animals were regularly used in experiments, governments had set up laws protecting people's furry and feathered friends. The first American animal cruelty law was enacted in 1641 in the Massachusetts Bay Colony, an English settlement in the area of North America that is now Boston, Massachusetts. Nearly two centuries later, in 1821, Maine passed the first state anticruelty law, which forbade people from beating horses or cattle.

Ten years later, British scientist Marshall Hall (1790–1857) proposed five principles that he thought should govern animal experiments. His principles were as follows:

- Scientists should not do any research if the information could be gathered by observation alone.
- Each experiment should have a clear purpose.
- Scientists should be aware of the work of researchers before them to avoid repeating the same experiments.
- Experiments should be done in a way that minimizes suffering to the animals.
- Tests should be designed to provide clear results so that they don't need to be repeated.

Although the scientific community didn't pay Hall much attention at the time, after his death in 1857, his ideas were used as the basis for both the British Animals (Scientific Procedures) Act and the U.S. Animal Welfare Act (AWA).

In 1866, a wealthy aristocrat named Henry Bergh (1811–1888) founded the American Society for the Prevention of Cruelty to

Animals (ASPCA), the first animal protection organization in the Western Hemisphere. The next year, Bergh convinced government officials in New York to pass a law making cruelty to animals a crime. That law became the model for future animal anticruelty laws.

Even as animal research became more common in the United States during the early part of the twentieth century, and general animal anticruelty laws were enacted, no one seemed to care much for the welfare of experiment subjects. That changed in 1966, with the publication of an article in *Life* magazine. The article was titled "Concentration Camps for Lost and Stolen Pets." It featured pictures of malnourished, sick-looking dogs. Its vivid pictures showed Americans the shocking conditions in which animals lived while waiting to be sold by dealers to research labs. The American people were outraged. In response to the public outcry, the U.S. government passed the Animal Welfare Act (AWA) to protect animals used in research.

The AWA requires that companies consider alternatives to animal research. When they do use animals, research laboratories must minimize pain and distress and treat those animals humanely. However, the AWA doesn't protect all animals used in research. In fact, the act doesn't include protection for rats and mice, which make up most of the experiment subjects.

Europe has also passed regulations on animal testing. Since 2003, no cosmetic can be sold in the European Union (EU, a group of twenty-seven European countries that includes France, Germany, Spain, and Sweden) if it contains ingredients that were tested on animals (provided that no alternatives to animal testing exist). In 2009, the EU will have a complete ban on animal testing in place.

MYTHS AND FACTS

MYTH Animals do not feel pain, so they don't experience any discomfort during experiments.

FACT Research finds that animals can feel pain, but many scientists use pain-relieving medicine (anesthesia) during experiments so that the animals feel as little pain as possible.

MYTH Scientists don't care about animals—they simply view animals as test subjects.

FACT Responsible scientists do care very much about the animals they test. There is a growing movement among researchers to conduct experiments with as few animals as possible and as humanely as possible.

MYTH Animal tests are the only way to learn whether new medications are safe.

FACT Today, scientists have come up with many new methods to test medications and chemicals, such as artificial human tissues and computer models. However, animal experiments remain an important part of the product-testing process.

Chapter Three

THE ARGUMENT FOR ANIMAL TESTING

It was the summer of 1952. At a time when children should have been outdoors playing stickball and packing up for summer camp, many were stuck indoors. Parents were terrified that their children would catch polio, a crippling disease that was raging across the country. Children who did get polio often ended up on crutches, in wheelchairs, or worse still, confined to a huge metal cylinder called an iron lung to help them breathe. In 1952, polio infected nearly sixty thousand Americans.

Before the decade was through, American physician Jonas Salk (1914–1995) announced that he had created a vaccine against polio. The vaccine used a killed version of the polio virus to protect

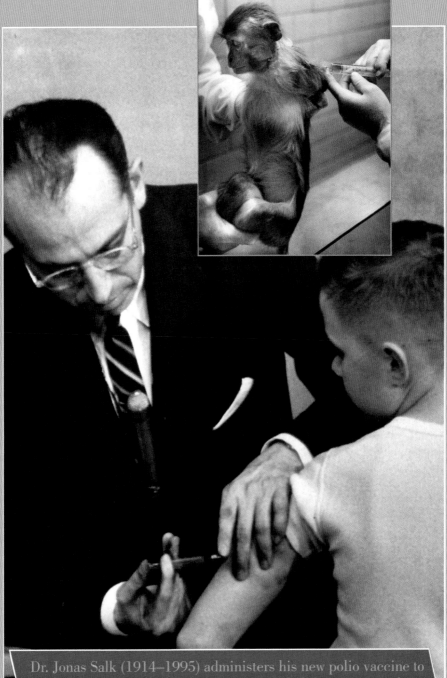

Dr. Jonas Salk (1914–1995) administers his new polio vaccine to a boy. The polio vaccine was made possible by tests on monkeys *(insert)* and other animals.

children against the disease. On the heels of Salk's discovery, a Polish doctor, Albert Sabin (1906–1993) introduced a live but weakened version of the polio vaccine. When people received Sabin's vaccine, they were protected from polio for life. These vaccines were made possible by experiments using monkeys, rats, and mice. By the mid-1990s, thanks to widespread vaccination, polio had been wiped out in the United States.

Polio wasn't the only disease children had to fear many years ago. Diphtheria, pertussis, tuberculosis, measles, and mumps were all deadly at one time. Today, they are almost nonexistent in America because of vaccines. Without animals, those vaccines could never have been developed.

Other lifesaving treatments that owe their development to animal testing include the following:

- Antibiotics, which treat bacterial infections
- Insulin, a treatment for people with diabetes, and methods to deliver insulin (such as a skin patch) so that diabetics don't have to inject themselves with a needle every day
- Open-heart surgery and organ transplant surgeries, as well as drugs to prevent people who receive a transplant from rejecting their new organ
- Medications to treat AIDS and cancer
- Drugs that slow memory loss in people with Alzheimer's disease (a disorder of the brain)
- Statin drugs, which help reduce the build-up of a fat-like substance called cholesterol in the blood and reduce the risks of heart attacks
- New spinal cord treatments to help return movement to people who have been paralyzed from an injury
- Drugs, such as medications to reduce depression, to help people with mental illness lead more normal lives

These treatments, which were tested on animals first, together have saved the lives of millions of people.

 Canine Friends

They may have fur on the outside, but on the inside, animals are a lot more like humans than you may realize. Many of the same diseases that sicken humans, including heart disease and cancer, also affect animals. Scientists can study these diseases in animals to learn more about how to treat them in humans.

Take the disease narcolepsy, for example. This condition causes people to fall asleep in the middle of the day—often in the middle of a conversation, or at another very inappropriate time. Narcolepsy is both embarrassing and dangerous. Imagine what would happen if a person fell asleep without warning while driving a car!

In the 1970s, researchers at Stanford University in California discovered that people's four-legged best friends—dogs—also fall prey to narcolepsy. They noticed that some dogs have the same sleepy symptoms as humans. By studying these narcoleptic dogs, researchers found a defect in the gene that causes narcolepsy, and they were able to develop new drugs to treat the condition in humans.

Another disease dogs share with humans is diabetes, one form of which occurs when the body doesn't make enough of the hormone insulin. As a result, the level of sugar in the blood (glucose) rises too high. At one time, diabetes was a fatal disease. Then, in the 1920s, doctors Frederick Banting (1891–1941) and Charles H. Best (1899–1978) discovered that giving insulin to dogs with diabetes could treat the condition. The insulin itself was once taken from the pancreas of pigs and cows. Today, people who are born with diabetes can live full lives, thanks to the animals that made diabetes research and treatment possible.

Why Scientists Need Animal Testing

No scientist sets out to test medications or treatments on animals with the goal of harming the animals or making them suffer.

Researchers Charles H. Best (1899–1978) and Frederick Banting (1891–1941) pose at Toronto University with a diabetic dog—one of the first to receive the hormone insulin. Their testing of insulin on dogs helped them discover that diabetes is treatable.

Instead, they name many reasons why animal testing is so important, including the following:

- It would not be morally right to test new treatments on humans because people could get sick or even die during the tests.
- Animals are very much like humans, so they can help us learn about human diseases and find new treatments for both human and animal illnesses.
- Animals can help medical students perfect their skills before trying them out on human patients.
- Testing animals saves money and time because it prevents scientists from having to test treatments that don't work.

According to surveys, most people agree on the importance of animal testing. About 65 percent of Americans support the use of animals in research that helps scientists learn how to treat disease, according to the Humane Society. People are especially accepting of animal testing when its purpose is to study deadly diseases, such as cancer.

Chapter Four

THE ARGUMENT AGAINST ANIMAL TESTING

F or almost as long as animal testing has existed, there have been people opposed to its practice. When the antivivisection movement began in Europe in the 1800s, people there started protesting against animal testing. Eventually, the movement spread to the United States and helped lead to the passage of animal protection and anti-cruelty laws.

There are two wings to the animal protection movement: animal welfare groups, such as the ASPCA and Humane Society, and animal rights groups, such as People for the Ethical Treatment of Animals (PETA) and the Animal Liberation Front (ALF). Animal welfare groups work to protect the safety and well-being of animals. Animal rights

Members of the organization People for the Ethical Treatment of Animals (PETA) often hold protests against animal testing.

Radical Animal Rights Groups

Not all animal activists have been engaged in peaceful protest. Some have used controversial methods—even violence—to fight for animal rights.

A group known as the Animal Liberation Front (ALF) was established in the 1970s with the goal of saving as many animals as possible, by any method possible. Their methods include destroying the offices of facilities that conduct animal research. In 1999, the ALF caused $750,000 in damage to offices and equipment at the University of Minnesota in Minneapolis, where researchers were using animals to study cancer and Alzheimer's disease. The ALF's tactics are so radical that the Federal Bureau of Investigation (FBI) considers the organization's members to be domestic terrorists.

Less radical, but still controversial, is the organization People for the Ethical Treatment of Animals (PETA). This group not only protests animal testing but also the use of animals for all purposes, from the circus to horse-drawn carriages. Cofounder and president Ingrid Newkirk was quoted in a *Time* article in June 2006 as saying that there was no difference between the suffering of a child and that of an animal. "A rat is a pig is a dog is a boy," she said.

groups believe that animals should have exactly the same rights as humans do and should not be used by humans for any purpose.

Animal activism reached its peak in the already politically charged 1970s. In the early part of that decade, Americans were caught up in protests against the Vietnam War. Protesters also took to the streets to oppose the Draize test and animal testing in general. In 1979, an activist named Henry Spira (1927–1998) launched a campaign against the Draize test, called the Coalition Against Animal Blinding Tests. Spira's group took out a full-page ad in the *New York Times* that asked, "How many rabbits has Revlon blinded for beauty's sake?" He challenged Revlon (a cosmetics company) to donate $750,000 over three years to research alternatives to the Draize test.

The company eventually agreed, and it set up a research program at Rockefeller University in New York City. Other cosmetics companies did likewise. They established a $1 million fund, which in 1980 helped to create the Center for Alternatives to Animal Testing (CAAT) at Johns Hopkins University in Baltimore, Maryland. This group works with scientists and the government to find ways to replace animals in drug and product testing, as well as in education.

The Ethics of Animal Testing

At the center of the animal rights debate is the idea that animals feel pain and have the right to be treated humanely. Activists say that experiments force animals to endure a lot of pain, stress, and anxiety, just to ensure that products are safe for human use. What's more, animals cannot speak for themselves or give their consent to participate in experiments.

There is no question that many of the tests performed are tough on the animals. Animals in research labs are exposed to substances that irritate their skin and cause birth defects, cancer, and even death. Lab animals are often kept in cages with wire grid floors where they have little room to move around. After the experiments are finished, animals are often put to death.

Problems with Animal Tests

Are animal tests the best way to evaluate new medicines and other products? Some people say that they are not.

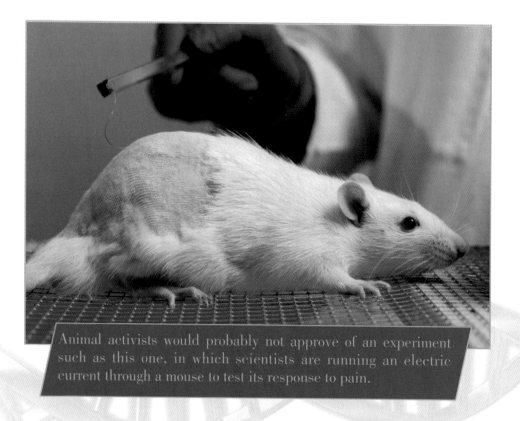

Animal activists would probably not approve of an experiment such as this one, in which scientists are running an electric current through a mouse to test its response to pain.

They argue that, even though humans and many animals are biologically similar, they are not exactly the same. Therefore, an animal's response to a chemical may not exactly mimic the response of a human. In 2006, scientists in London, England, injected six human volunteers with an experimental treatment for rheumatoid arthritis and multiple sclerosis. Though the drug had been tested on mice, rats, rabbits, and monkeys with no obvious problems, the humans had a violent reaction, which caused their heads to balloon in size. Because testing on humans is limited, there isn't good information on humans to compare against the data from animals. Some people say that many animal tests were developed so long ago that no one is sure whether they still work well today. Here are a few of the arguments for animal testing, and the response by animal activists:

FOR ANIMAL TESTS	AGAINST ANIMAL TESTS
Animal testing is necessary because it saves lives.	Many of the drugs that were developed through animal testing could have been tested without the use of animals.
People must test products on animals to prevent causing harm to humans.	Animals have the same right as humans to live and not suffer.
Animals make good models for disease and treatments because they are similar to humans biologically.	Animals are not exactly the same as humans and may not respond in the same way to treatments.
Laws are in place to protect animals from suffering during experiments.	No matter how careful researchers are, animals can still feel pain and stress from being kept in cages and subjected to tests.

People on both sides of the debate are sure that they are right about their stand on animal testing. Until scientists can eliminate the need for animal experiments, these arguments are likely to continue. Thanks to research into alternatives to animal tests, the day might come when laboratories do not need to use a single animal.

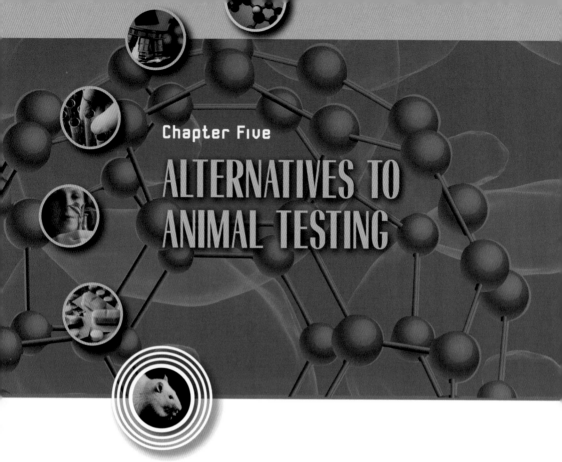

Chapter Five

ALTERNATIVES TO ANIMAL TESTING

(M) ost scientists today want to find ways to use fewer animals, or none at all, in experiments. Their effort stems from an idea called the "three Rs," which was developed by zoologist William M. S. Russell and microbiologist Rex L. Burch of the Universities Federation for Animal Welfare in Great Britain. In their 1959 book, *The Principles of Humane Experimental Technique*, Russell and Burch described the "three Rs" as follows:

- **Replacement:** Use alternatives to animal testing.
- **Reduction:** Reduce the number of animals in each experiment.

○- **Refinement:** Improve experiments to reduce animal suffering.

Many of these techniques are already in use today. Others are still being developed. The next descriptions include some examples of how scientists today are using the "three Rs."

Replacement

Scientists are finding many new ways to test products without animals. They have created artificial skin and organs that can mimic the response of a human's or animal's body. A few of the new techniques that are helping to replace animals in experiments include:

○- **Artificial skin.** Scientists in Europe have created a substance that looks and acts like human skin. To make this artificial skin, first they take human cells left over from plastic surgery operations. Then, they grow those cells in a gel made from collagen, a type of protein found in skin. The reconstructed skin looks and acts like real skin. Scientists can use this "skin" to test sunscreens and cosmetics to see whether they might cause irritation to or damage real skin. They can also add a chemical called MTT to the artificial skin. When this chemical turns skin blue, it means that the skin is alive and has not been damaged by the test substance. Scientists have also developed artificial eyes to test eye irritation and artificial lung cells to study drugs that people inhale.

○- **Computer modeling.** Scientists believe that computers may be able to predict the effects of drugs on the human body. Researchers program into a computer the information they already know about human cells and the drug being tested. Then, the computer uses a mathematical formula to

Scientists are creating artificial skin to help them test chemicals without using live animals.

predict what effects the drug might have on cells, organs, and other tissues.

- **Cell cultures.** Scientists can test chemicals and drugs on cells in a test tube to see how the cells respond, without having to actually put the substance in the body. To see how the whole body might respond to the chemical, scientists can take cells from many different organs, such as the kidney, liver, and stomach.
- **Toxicogenomics.** This very new branch of science studies how human genes interact with substances such as drugs and the environment to lead to disease. Scientists use DNA microarrays (also called DNA chips), which are

This tool, called a microarray, helps scientists study how different genes might interact with chemicals. Instruments such as microarrays have helped to revolutionize drug development and clinical research.

slides made up of thousands of different tiny pieces of DNA. When a test chemical is placed on the DNA, it can show what effect that substance might have on the body.

These new methods and those that are currently being studied show potential in allowing researchers to test products without involving animals.

Reduction

With new methods of drug and chemical testing, the number of animals used in lab experiments has dropped by 50 percent,

The Rabbit Test

One of the best examples of how animals have been replaced in research is the so-called rabbit test. Many years ago, if a woman wanted to know whether she was pregnant, she would have had a lab test. During the test, lab workers would inject the woman's urine into a female rabbit. Then, they would test the rabbit's ovaries (the glands that produce eggs) for a certain change that occurs when women are pregnant. One rabbit would have to die for each pregnancy test that was done.

Today, the rabbit test has been replaced by a chemical test strip. Women can find out whether they are pregnant in a matter of seconds, without any animals being harmed.

Dr. Alan Goldberg, director of the Center for Alternatives to Animal Testing at Johns Hopkins University, told the *New York Times* in 2007. The following are just a few of the ways in which scientists are cutting back on the number of animal subjects:

- **Replacement eyes.** Several methods are allowing companies to use far fewer rabbits for the Draize eye test. One method uses cow and chicken eyeballs from animals that have already been killed in slaughterhouses. Another uses chicken eggs because the blood vessels in them are similar to those in human eyes.
- **Lymph node testing.** In the past, guinea pigs were often used to test allergic skin reactions to cosmetics and medications. A new test called local lymph node assay (LLNA) uses mice instead for the same purpose. The test looks at

how the mice's lymph nodes (small glands that are part of the immune system) respond to the drugs. The LLNA test uses far fewer animals and is less painful than the old allergy tests.

- **Skin tests.** A new test uses rat skin cells to see whether chemicals will burn the skin. Although some rats do have to be killed to get the cells, only one animal has to be killed, rather than the three animals that had to die for each chemical tested by the old methods.
- **Fever test.** In the 1970s, scientists used the pyrogen test to find out whether a substance contained bacteria that would cause a fever. They would inject the substance into rabbits and then take their temperature twenty-four hours later. Today, researchers use the limulus test instead. This test looks at the effect of bacteria on a sample of blood taken from a horseshoe crab.

More tests are being developed that will further reduce the number of animals used in experiments.

Refinement

If scientists cannot completely stop using animals in tests, then they can make the experience better for the animals. Here are some of the methods by which companies are refining their experimenting with animals:

- **Less pain.** Giving pain medication to lab animals can make uncomfortable experiments more bearable. Also, scientists have started to use imaging scans, such as X-rays, to see what effects a substance is having in the animals' bodies without having to cut the animals open.
- **Smaller doses.** A new version of the Draize test uses one-tenth of the test substance that was used in the past to

reduce damage to the rabbit's eye. Also, scientists are trying to test chemicals that are less irritating to the rabbits.

- **Better living conditions.** Providing bigger cages, other animals to play with, and toys can improve life for animals that have to live in laboratories.
- **Different animals.** Researchers are using fewer mammals (mice and rabbits) and more invertebrates (animals without a backbone) and microscopic organisms (such as bacteria), which are thought to feel less pain.

Ending Cosmetics Testing

Although many Americans say they are in favor of using animals to test the safety of medicines and chemicals, most are against using animals to test products that are not used for health purposes. In one study, 60 percent of people surveyed said they opposed the use of animals in cosmetics testing, according to the Humane Society.

As mentioned previously, Europe has already begun the move to ban cosmetics testing on animals. As of 2003, no cosmetic can be sold in the European Union (EU) if it, or its ingredients, were tested on animals (provided that no alternatives to animal testing exist). In 2009, the EU will launch a total ban on cosmetics testing.

Today, cosmetics companies in the United States are also phasing out animal testing. Many have already stopped testing their products on animals. Some are using human volunteers instead.

In 1989, Revlon became the first cosmetics company to end all of its animal testing. Avon and Mary Kay announced soon after that they were also ending animal testing. Gillette stopped testing its products in 1996, and it donates $100,000 each year toward the development of alternative testing methods. L'Oréal and Procter & Gamble have each spent hundreds of millions of dollars to find alternatives to animal testing. Some companies, such as the Body Shop and Tom's of Maine, label their products "Cruelty-free" or "Against animal testing."

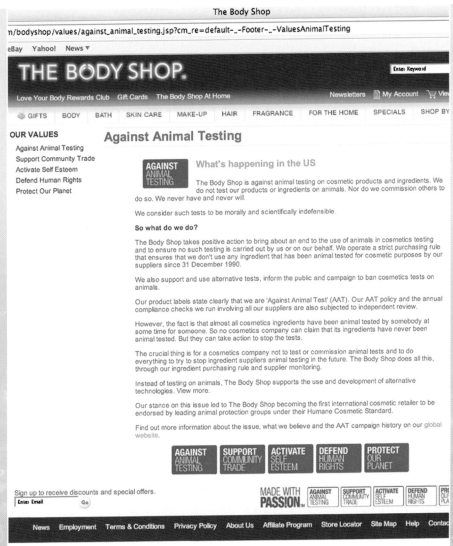

The Body Shop's Web site (http://www.thebodyshop.com) includes this page that describes the company's values against animal testing. The Body Shop and many other companies that sell cosmetics label their products "Cruelty-free" or "Against animal testing."

What Does "Cruelty–Free" Mean?

When you pick up a jar of hand lotion or a bottle of perfume and see the words "Cruelty-free" or "Not tested on animals," it may sound positive, but what do those words really mean? The meanings are not always clear.

"Cruelty-free" may mean that the company uses other methods besides animals to test its products. Or, it may mean that the company doesn't test products itself, but it might still buy from companies that do animal tests on either the finished product or the ingredients. To learn more about whether or not a product truly is cruelty-free, visit the Web site of In Defense of Animals (http://www.idausa.org/facts/crueltyfree.html) or other organizations that keep lists of animal-test-free products and companies.

Challenges to Reducing Animal Testing

Even as researchers are working hard to come up with new tests that use fewer or no animals, some laws are making it more difficult for companies to stop animal tests. The FDA does not allow any new drug to reach store shelves without first being tested on animals. For many studies of drug safety, the FDA won't accept any alternative to animal testing. The agency is worried that if it switches from testing methods that have already been proven to work, people might get sick or even die during the alternative tests.

The Environmental Protection Agency (EPA) is a U.S. government agency whose job is to make sure that the air is safe to breathe and the water is safe to drink, among other responsibilities. It calls for many types of animal tests, for example, to find

Members of the environmental organization Greenpeace demonstrate in Rome, Italy, against the use of chemicals in commercial products that are designed for children.

out what might happen if people are exposed to lead, mercury, and other dangerous substances in the air or water.

Both in Europe and the United States, governments have discovered that many products already in use have not yet been tested well enough. They are requiring that companies go back and test these products to make sure they're safe. In Europe, a law called REACH (Registration Evaluation and Authorization of Chemicals) is making companies gather safety information on about thirty thousand chemicals, from those used in automobiles to computers to children's toys, either produced or used in Europe. In 2001, the U.K. Medical Research Council figured out that this new law would probably involve using more than thirteen million animals, as *Scientific American* reported in 2006.

In the United States, the government discovered back in the late 1990s that only about a quarter of one hundred thousand commonly used chemicals had safety information on them. Former vice president Al Gore introduced a new program, called the Chemical Right to Know Initiative, on Earth Day in 1998 to test thousands of these chemicals for safety. Under a part of this initiative is the High Production Volume (HPV) Challenge Program, where companies and manufacturers are "challenged" to make available information about health and environmental effects of chemicals made in or imported into the United States in the largest quantities. The HPV chemicals are those that are made in or imported into the United States in amounts of 1 million pounds (453,592 kilograms) or more each year. These tests, however, may involve an estimated one million animals.

The Move to Stop Animal Testing

Despite the continuing need for animal tests, scientists are making great progress in finding other methods for testing chemicals and drugs. In recent years, the U.S. government has gotten involved in the efforts to reduce animal testing. The National Institutes of Health has set up a special agency to look into alternatives to animal tests. The Interagency Coordinating Committee on the Validation of Alternative Methods (ICCVAM) helps approve new methods for government agencies that do animal testing. Any possible new test must be checked by its scientists and be shown to work in laboratories before the government can approve it.

Researchers say that it is impossible to eliminate all animal tests, at least for now. However, every day they are finding new ways to decrease the number of animals in tests and reduce the suffering of those animals that are used in experiments and testing for biomedical research, education, and product safety.

GLOSSARY

AIDS A disease caused by the human immunodeficiency virus (HIV) that weakens the immune system.

Alzheimer's disease A disease of the brain that leads to memory loss and confusion.

anesthesia Medicine that relieves pain. Anesthesia is often used to prevent a patient from feeling pain during surgery.

cholesterol A fat-like substance that can build up in the arteries and block blood flow through them.

collagen A strong protein that helps strengthen skin, tendons, and bone.

diabetes A disease in which the body either does not make enough of the hormone insulin or cannot use it properly. As a result, sugar (glucose) builds up in the blood.

diphtheria A serious infection of the throat, nose, and lungs.

dissect To cut apart an animal to study its organs and tissues.

DNA Deoxyribonucleic acid, the genetic material found in each cell of the body.

Draize test A test that is performed on rabbits to find out if a substance damages or irritates the eyes.

euthanize To kill an animal or individual in as humane a way as possible.

genes Segments of DNA that carry the instructions the cells of the body need to do their jobs.

insulin A hormone made by the pancreas that helps the cells use sugar from food for energy.

measles A very infectious disease that causes fever and a skin rash.

mumps A disease that causes swelling in the neck.

narcolepsy A disease that causes people to fall asleep at unusual times, often during the day.

paralyzed Unable to move.

pertussis A respiratory disease, also known as whooping cough, that causes people to make a "whooping" sound when they cough.

polio A disease that affects the spinal cord and can leave a person paralyzed.

racism The notion that one's ethnicity is superior.

toxicogenomics The study of how genes respond to toxic substances.

tuberculosis A disease that is catching and that especially affects the lungs; it is characterized by fever, cough, and difficulty in breathing.

vivisection Cutting open a living animal for scientific study.

American Anti-Vivisection Society
801 Old York Road, #204
Jenkintown, PA 19046
(215) 887-0816
Web site: http://www.aavs.org
This nonprofit society was formed in 1883. Its goal is to end the
  use of all animals in scientific research.

American Association for the Advancement of Science (AAAS)
1200 New York Avenue NW
Washington, DC 20005
(202) 326-6400
Web site: http://www.aaas.org
The AAAS is an international nonprofit organization that works to
  promote integrity in science and provides a voice for science
  on societal issues.

American Association for Laboratory Animal Science (AALAS)
9190 Crestwyn Hills Drive
Memphis, TN 38125
(901) 754-8620
Web site: http://www.aalas.org
The AALAS is devoted to the humane study and treatment of
  laboratory animals.

American Humane Association
63 Inverness Drive East
Englewood, CO 80112
(303) 792-9900
Web site: http://www.americanhumane.org

The American Humane Association is a network of people who
work toward preventing cruelty, abuse, neglect, and exploita-
tion of children and animals and to ensure their well-being.

Americans for Medical Progress
908 King Street, Suite 301
Alexandria, VA 22314
(703) 836-9595
Web site: http://www.amprogress.org
Americans for Medical Progress attempts to foster public
understanding of and support for the humane, necessary,
and valuable use of animals in medicine.

American Society for the Prevention of
Cruelty to Animals (ASPCA)
424 East 92nd Street
New York, NY 10128
(212) 876-7700
Web site: http://www.aspca.org
The ASPCA has been in existence since 1866. Since that time,
its goal has been to put an end to animal cruelty.

American Veterinary Medical Association (AVMA)
1931 North Meacham Road, Suite 100
Schaum, IL 60173-4360
(847) 925-8070
Web site: http://www.avma.org
A not-for-profit organization, the AVMA represents more than
seventy-six thousand veterinarians working in private and
corporate practice, government, industry, academic insti-
tutions, and uniformed services. Its mission is to improve
animal and human health and advance the science and art
of veterinary medicine, including its connection to public
health, biological science, and agriculture.

Animal Welfare Foundation of Canada
410 Bank Street, Suite 616
Ottawa, ON K2P 1Y8
Canada
Web site: http://www.awfc.ca/english/index.htm
The goal of this foundation is to protect animals in Canada
    from harm.

Association for Assessment and Accreditation of
    Laboratory Animal Care International (AAALAC)
5283 Corporate Drive, Suite 203
Frederick, MD 21703
(301) 696-9626
Web site: http://www.aaalac.org
AAALAC International is a private, nonprofit group that works
    toward the humane treament of animals in science through
    voluntary accreditation and assessment programs.

Canadian Association for Laboratory Animal Science
144 Front Street West, #640
Toronto, ON M5J 2L7
Canada
(416) 593-0268
Web site: http://www.calas-acsal.org
This Canadian organization promotes high standards of lab animal
    science to enhance animal well-being and care in research.

Canadian Council on Animal Care (CCAC)
130 Albert Street, Suite 1510
Ottawa, ON K1P 5G4
Canada
(613) 238-4031
Web site: http://www.ccac.ca/en/CCAC_Main.htm
Founded in 1968, the CCAC oversees the use of animals in
    Canadian research.

Foundation for Biomedical Research
818 Connecticut Avenue NW, Suite 900
Washington, DC 20006
(202) 457-0654
Web site: http://www.fbresearch.org
This is the oldest organization in the United States that is
    devoted to promoting humane animal-based research.

Humane Society of the United States
2100 L Street NW
Washington, DC 20037
(202) 452-1100
Web site: http://www.hsus.org
The Humane Society was founded in 1954, and today it is the
    largest animal protection organization in the country.

Johns Hopkins University Center for
    Alternatives to Animal Testing
111 Market Place, Suite 840
Baltimore, MD 21202-6709
(410) 223-1692
Web site: http://caat.jhsph.edu
This center is part of the Johns Hopkins University Bloomberg
    School of Public Health and is dedicated to improving health
    for people and animals and finding alternatives to animal
    testing without compromising research.

Scientists Center for Animal Welfare (SCAW)
7833 Walker Drive, Suite 410
Greenbelt, MD 20770
(301) 345-3500
Web site: http://www.scaw.com
This organization promotes the best animal research and testing
    practices as possible to improve the well-being of all animals
    used in teaching, testing, and research.

U.S. Food and Drug Administration (FDA)
5600 Fishers Lane
Rockville, MD 20857-0001
(888) INFO-FDA (463-6332)
Web site: http://www.fda.gov
This government agency ensures that food products and drugs
are as safe as possible. The FDA is responsible for ensuring
that cosmetics are safe and properly labeled, and it has
oversight of the Federal Food, Drug, and Cosmetic Act and
regulations.

Web Sites

Due to the changing nature of Internet links, Rosen Publishing
has developed an online list of Web sites related to the subject
of this book. This site is updated regularly. Please use this link
to access the list:

http://www.rosenlinks.com/sas/ante

FOR FURTHER READING

Haugen, David, ed. *Animal Experimentation* (Opposing Viewpoints). Farmington Hills, MI: Greenhaven Press, 2006.

Hile, Kevin. *Animal Rights* (Point/Counterpoint). New York, NY: Chelsea House Publishers, 2004.

Judson, Karen. *Animal Testing* (Open for Debate). New York, NY: Benchmark Books, 2006.

Newkirk, Ingrid. *50 Awesome Ways Kids Can Help Animals: Fun and Easy Ways to Be a Kind Kid*. Rev. ed. New York, NY: Grand Central Publishing, 2006.

Noyes, Deborah. *One Kingdom: Our Lives with Animals*. Boston, MA: Houghton Mifflin, 2006.

Padilla, Michael J., Ioannis Miaoulis, and Martha Cyr. *Science Explorer: Animals*. Upper Saddle River, NJ: Pearson Prentice Hall, 2004.

Ritter, Christie. *Animal Rights* (Essential Viewpoints). Edina, MN: ABDO Publishing, 2008.

Taylor, Barbara. *Amazing Animal Facts*. London, England: Lorenz Books, 2006.

Trumbauer, Lisa. *Exploring Animal Rights and Animal Welfare*. Westport, CT: Greenwood Publishing Group, 2002.

Yount, Lisa. *Animal Rights* (Library in a Book). Rev. ed. New York, NY: Facts on File, 2007.

BIBLIOGRAPHY

BBC.com. "Animal Experiments." August 17, 2004. Retrieved December 15, 2007 (http://www.bbc.co.uk/science/hottopics/animalexperiments/index.shtml).

Birnbaum, Jesse. "Just Too Beastly for Words." Time.com, June 13, 2006. Retrieved February 29, 2008 (http://www.time.com/time/magazine/article/0,9171,973243-1,00.html).

Brooman, Simon, and Dr. Debbie Legge. *Law Relating to Animals*. London, England: Cavendish Publishing, Limited, 1999.

Carvajal, Doreen. "Cosmetics Makers Need Artificial Skin to Eliminate Tests on Animals." *New York Times* News Service, November 20, 2007.

Descartes, René, Elizabeth S. Haldine, and G. R. T. Ross. *The Philosophical Works of Descartes, Volume II*. Cambridge, England: Cambridge University Press, 1967.

Economist.com. "Humane League." August 30, 2007. Retrieved December 12, 2007 (http://www.economist.com/science/displaystory.cfm?story_id=9719666).

English, Rebecca. "Elephant Man Couldn't Resist Drug Test Money." *Daily Mail*, March 20, 2006. Retrieved May 8, 2008 (http://www.dailymail.co.uk/pages/live/articles/news/news.html?in_article_id=380395&in_page_id=1770&in_a_source).

Goldberg, Alan, and Thomas Hartung. "Protecting More Than Animals." *Scientific American*, Vol. 294, No. 1, January 2006, pp. 84–91.

Goodman, Brenda. "Coca-Cola and PepsiCo Agree to Curb Animal Tests." *New York Times*, May 31, 2007. Retrieved December 12, 2007 (http://www.nytimes.com/2007/05/31/business/31testing.html).

Humane Society of the United States. "Frequently Asked Questions About Animals in Research." Retrieved December 15, 2007 (http://www.hsus.org/animals_in_research/general_information_on_animal_research/frequently_asked_questions_about_animals_in_research.html).

Humane Society of the United States. "An Overview of Animal Testing Issues." Retrieved December 20, 2007 (http://www.hsus.org/web-files/PDF/ARI/ARIS_An_Overview_Of_Animal_Testing_Issues.pdf).

Humane Society of the United States. "Public Attitudes to Animal Research." Retrieved December 28, 2007 (http://www.hsus.org/animals_in_research/general_information_on_animal_research/overview_of_the_issues/b_public_attitudes_to_animal_research.html).

Kiefer, Heather Mason. "Americans Unruffled by Animal Testing." Gallup, May 25, 2004. Retrieved December 12, 2007 (http://www.gallup.com/poll/11767/Americans-Unruffled-Animal-Testing.aspx).

Merali, Zeeya. "Human Skin to Replace Animal Tests." *New Scientist*, Vol. 195, No. 2614, July 28, 2007, p. 38.

Orlans, F. Barbara. *In the Name of Science: Issues in Responsible Animal Experimentation*. New York, NY: Oxford University Press, 1993.

Zurlo, Joanne, Deborah Rudacille, and Alan M. Goldberg. "Animals and Alternatives in Testing: History, Science, and Ethics." Johns Hopkins University Center for Alternatives to Animal Testing. Retrieved December 30, 2007 (http://caat.jhsph.edu/publications/animal_alternatives/chapter3.htm).

INDEX

About the Author

Stephanie Watson is a writer based in Atlanta, Georgia. She is a regular contributor to several online and print health publications, and she has written or contributed to more than two dozen books, including *The Genetics of Obesity, Fast Food* (What's in Your Food? Recipe for Disaster), *and Biotechnology: Changing Life Through Science.*

Photo Credits

Cover, pp. 16, 32, 35 © Getty Images; cover (inset) © www.istockphotos.com/Johannes Hloch; pp. 5, 17 © Shutterstock; p. 8 © Gard/Phanie/Photo Researchers; pp. 9, 29 ©Time-Life Pictures/Getty Images (2 photos); p. 10 © Bob Daemmrich/ The Image Works; p. 13 © Popperfoto/Getty Images; p. 19 © Nigel Cattlin/Photo Researchers; p. 20 © Science Source/Photo Researchers; p. 24 © National Geographic/Getty Images; p. 38 © Philippe Psaila/Photo Researchers; pp. 42, 49 © AP Photo; p. 43 © Seth Resnick/Getty Images.

Designer: Evelyn Horovicz; Cover Designer: Nelson Sá
Editor: Kathy Kuhtz Campbell; Photo Researcher: Marty Levick